Basic Accounting I
Wise Guide

AAT Level 2 Certificate in Accounting

Image of owl © Eric Isselée-Fotolia.com

Published by Osborne Books Limited, Unit 1B Everoak Estate, Bromyard Road, Worcester WR
Tel 01905 748071, Email books@osbornebooks.co.uk, Website www.osbornebooks.co.uk

Printed and bound by Mimeo, UK.

ISBN 978 1905777 877

how to use this Wise Guide

This Wise Guide has been designed to supplement your Tutorial and Workbook. It has two main aims:

- to reinforce your learning as you study your course
- to help you prepare for your online assessment

This Wise Guide is organised in the specific topic areas listed on pages 4 and 5. These individual topic areas have been designed to cover the main areas of study, concentrating on specific areas of difficulty. There is also an index at the back to help you find the areas you are studying or revising.

The Owl symbolises wisdom, and acts as your tutor, introducing and explaining topics. Please let us know if he is doing his job properly. If you have feedback on this material please email books@osbornebooks.co.uk

Thank you and good luck with your study and revision.

Osborne Books

REVISION TIPS

'OWL' stands for: Observe Write Learn

There are a number of well-known ways in which you can remember information:

▪ *You can remember what it looks like on the page. Diagrams, lists, mind-maps, colour coding for different types of information, all help you **observe** and remember.*

▪ *You can remember what you **write** down. Flash cards, post-it notes around the bathroom mirror, notes on a mobile phone all help. It is the process of writing which fixes the information in the brain.*

▪ *You can **learn** by using this Wise Guide. Read through each topic carefully and then prepare your own written version on flash cards, post-it notes, wall charts – anything that you can see regularly.*

▪ *Lastly, give yourself **chill out** time, your brain a chance to recover and the information time to sink in. Promise yourself treats when you have finished studying – a drink, chocolate, a work out. Relax! And pass.*

list of contents

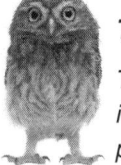

THE ACCOUNTING PROCESS

This process involves the recording of financial transactions, based on information taken from financial documents, eg invoices, credit notes. The process records transactions such as . . .

- *purchases*
- *sales*
- *payment of expenses*

this process follows a number of steps . . .

▪ the document is first recorded in a book of prime entry, eg a day book

▪ the data is then entered in ledger (double-entry) accounts

▪ and is summarised in a list of accounts – the trial balance – which provides owners and management with financial information

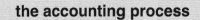

the accounting process

FINANCIAL TRANSACTIONS	a sale, a purchase, a payment
▼	
FINANCIAL DOCUMENTS	an invoice, a credit note, a remittance advice
▼	
BOOKS OF PRIME ENTRY	where the document is first recorded in the books, eg a day book
▼	
DOUBLE-ENTRY ACCOUNTS	double-entry ledger accounts
▼	
TRIAL BALANCE	a listing of the ledger accounts

2 Double-entry

THE DOUBLE-ENTRY SYSTEM

This can be a pain to get to grips with in the first place as it seems very complicated, with so many things to remember. But once you have got it worked out, it is very straightforward.

So remember:

- for every transaction there are entries in **two accounts**
- each account has two sides:
  - a **debit** (often written as **dr**) side on the **left** (UK drivers **dr**ive on the **left**)
  - a **credit** (often written as **cr**) side on the **right** (UK drivers **cr**ash on the **right**)
- the accounts are often set out in the form of a 'T' with the account name at the top
- each transaction has a debit entry in one account and a credit entry in the other account, as shown on the next page

debit (dr)	Account name	credit (cr)
debit entry		

debit (dr)	Account name	credit (cr)
		credit entry

EXAMPLE:

Buying a **computer** for £3,000 and paying by electronic transfer from the **bank**.

debit (dr)	Computer Account	credit (cr)
Bank	3,000	

debit (dr)	Bank Account	credit (cr)
	Computer	3,000

EXAMPLE

Receiving £5,000 cash from **sales** and paying it into the **bank**.

debit (dr)	Sales Account	credit (cr)
	Bank	5,000

debit (dr)	Bank Account	credit (cr)
Sales	5,000	

RULES OF DOUBLE-ENTRY

- for every transaction there are entries in two accounts

- for every transaction there is one debit entry and one credit entry

- in the case of the bank account the entries can be either debit or credit

- the name included in each entry is the name of the other account

should the account have a debit entry or a credit entry?

This is the big problem.

It becomes easy once you have learnt the basic rules that state which type of account normally has debit entries and which type of account has credit entries.

There are various ways in which you can do this, and when learning about double-entry you should be guided by your tutor.

When you have got a good grasp of debits and credits you may find it useful to use the 'Memory aids' section on page 84.

One useful method of learning the rules is to memorise this chart.

debit (dr)	credit (cr)
Purchases	Revenue
Expenses	Liabilities and Capital
Assets	Sales

more detail about debits (left-hand side)

debit (dr)	credit (cr)
Purchases - eg inventory (stock)	Revenue (ie income)
Expenses - eg wages	Liabilities - items owed and Capital
Assets - items owned	Sales

■ Purchases
Purchases in this case are purchases of goods which a business sells.

■ Expenses
These are the running expenses of a business, wages for example.

■ Assets
Assets are items that a business **owns**: vehicles, computers, money in the bank.
Another asset is money **owed to** a business by customers (trade receivables).

All these items will appear as **debits** – on the left-hand side of the double-entry
accounts.

more detail about credits (right-hand side)

debit (dr)	credit (cr)
Purchases - eg inventory (stock)	Revenue (ie income)
Expenses - eg wages	Liabilities - items owed and Capital
Assets - items owned	Sales

- **Revenue**
  Revenue is the term used for the income items of a business, for example rent received from letting out an office.

- **Liabilities**
  These are items a business owes, for example bank loans and money to suppliers (trade payables). It also includes **Capital**, the money put in by the owner(s).

- **Sales**
  This is the money received from the sales of products or services.

All these items will appear as **credits** – on the right-hand side.

3   The accounting equation

assets = capital + liabilities

*The principle which underlies double-entry bookkeeping is the **accounting equation**.*

When you understand this principle, the way in which double-entry works will become much clearer.

starting a business

If you start a business you will have a shopping list for things you will need to get hold of. These are **assets.** But you will need to provide money for all this:

- with your own money – this is **capital –** the owner's investment and profits
- you can borrow money and buy on credit – these are **liabilities** – items that you owe

The **accounting equation** is just common sense:

what you buy and what you own = what you have invested plus what you have borrowed and owe.

This can be put another way: **assets = capital + liabilities**

HOW THE ACCOUNTING EQUATION WORKS

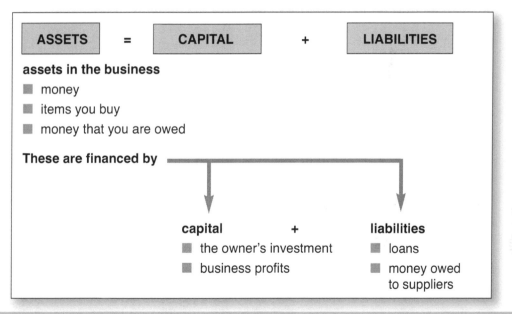

| ASSETS | = | CAPITAL | + | LIABILITIES |

assets in the business

- money
- items you buy
- money that you are owed

These are financed by

capital +
- the owner's investment
- business profits

liabilities
- loans
- money owed to suppliers

the accounting equation and double-entry – so what?

You may well ask what the accounting equation has to do with double-entry. Read through the two pages that follow this one you will see that as time passes and financial transactions are made, the double-entry that you carry out makes sure that the accounting equation always balances exactly.

RULES FOR DOUBLE-ENTRY TRANSACTIONS

First of all you will need to remember how changes in assets, capital and liabilities are recorded in the double-entry system:

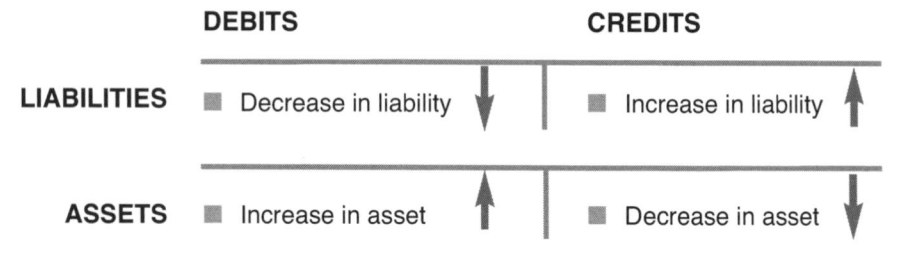

	DEBITS	**CREDITS**
LIABILITIES	■ Decrease in liability ↓	■ Increase in liability ↑
ASSETS	■ Increase in asset ↑	■ Decrease in asset ↓

Now you can apply these rules to some examples, as shown on the next few pages.

EXAMPLE

The owner invests £100,000 of capital in the business and pays it into the bank account.

The double-entry account entries are:

- ■ debit bank account £100,000
- ■ credit capital account £100,000

This means you are:

- ■ increasing an asset (bank account) by £100,000 – a **debit**
- ■ increasing capital (capital account) by £100,000 – a **credit**

so what is the effect on the accounting equation?

- ■ The accounting equation still balances because all you have done is added the same amount of £100,000 to both sides:

| ASSETS
+ £100,000 | = | CAPITAL
+ £100,000 | + | LIABILITIES
no change |

EXAMPLE

The owner buys a **computer** for £15,000 and pays from the business **bank** account. The double-entry account entries are:

- **debit computer account** £15,000   **credit bank account** £15,000

This means you are:

- increasing an asset (computer account) by £15,000 – a **debit**
- decreasing an asset (bank account) by £15,000 – a **credit**

so what is the effect on the accounting equation?

- There is no change to the accounting equation because all you have done is swapped one asset (money in the bank) for another (a computer).
- There is no change to either capital or liabilities.

ASSETS + £15,000 – £15,000 = no change	=	CAPITAL no change	+	LIABILITIES no change

EXAMPLE

The owner pays a **supplier** invoice for £2,000 and transfers the money from the business **bank** account. The double-entry account entries are:

■ **debit supplier account** £2,000   ■ **credit bank account** £2,000

This means you are:

■ decreasing a liability (supplier account) by £2,000 – a **debit**

■ decreasing an asset (bank account) by £2,000 – a **credit**

so what is the effect on the accounting equation?

■ There is no change to the accounting equation because what you have done is to reduce both sides of the equation by the same amount of £2,000.

■ The accounting equation still balances.

ASSETS – £2,000	=	CAPITAL no change	+	LIABILITIES – £2,000

4   Capital and revenue

CAPITAL OR REVENUE EXPENSE?

In accounting you need to understand the difference between:

■ **Capital expense** – *payment for non-current (fixed) assets and the associated costs*

■ **Revenue expense** – *day-to-day running expenses*

Remember

■ a **current asset** is something owned by the business for the short term, eg inventory (stock), money in the bank

■ a **non-current (fixed) asset** is owned by the business for the long term, eg property, computers, vehicles

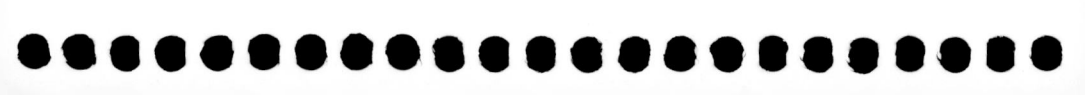

Capital expense includes:

- the **purchase cost** of non-current assets such as property, machinery and computers – ie items which are kept for the long term

- the **installation cost** of non-current assets such as property and machinery

- the **cost of improvement** (but not repair) of non-current assets, eg extending a property

- the **legal cost** of purchasing non-current assets such as property

Revenue expense is the day-to-day cost of running the business; it includes:

- **purchases** of inventory which will be re-sold or used in manufacturing

- **selling expenses** such as advertising and distribution

- **administration expenses** such as wages, power bills and stationery

- **repair and maintenance** of non-current assets, for example decorating, cleaning

CAPITAL OR REVENUE INCOME?

*In accounting you will also come across **capital income** and **revenue income** and you will need to know the difference between the two types of income:*

Capital income includes:

- money received from the sale of non-current assets such as property

- bank loans received

- extra capital invested by the business owner

Revenue income includes:

- money received from sales

- regular amounts received, eg rent received, commission received, settlement discounts

5 Financial documents

Financial documents result from financial transactions and are the basis of many of the entries into the accounting system.

*When dealing with documents you need first to sort out whether you are the **seller** or the **buyer**, and also whether you are **issuing** or **receiving** the documents. A typical sales transaction (ignoring any returns or refunds) looks like this:*

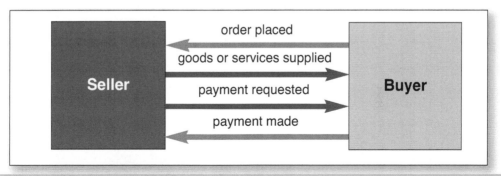

The MAIN FINANCIAL DOCUMENTS sent between the buyer and the seller are:

- **purchase order** – the details of an order placed by a buyer, eg product code and the quantity of the goods required

- **delivery note** – details of the goods (or services) supplied and sent out by the seller with the goods

- **invoice** – this is sent by the seller; it sets out how much has to be paid, when and on what terms

- **returns note** – sent out by the buyer with any goods returned to the seller (eg faulty or incorrect goods)

- **credit note** – sent by seller, reducing the amount owed by the buyer

- **statement of account** – sets out the amount owing by a buyer, sent out by the seller

- **remittance advice** – sent by the buyer, gives the seller the details of payment being made by the buyer

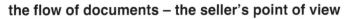

the flow of documents – the seller's point of view

This shows how various documents pass between the seller and the buyer at various stages in the transaction. It is set out from the **seller's** point of view.

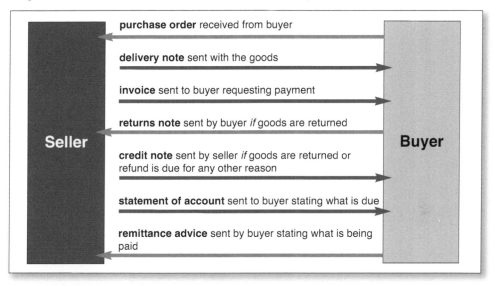

the flow of documents – the buyer's point of view

This shows how various documents pass between the buyer and the seller at various stages in the transaction. It is set out from the buyer's point of view.

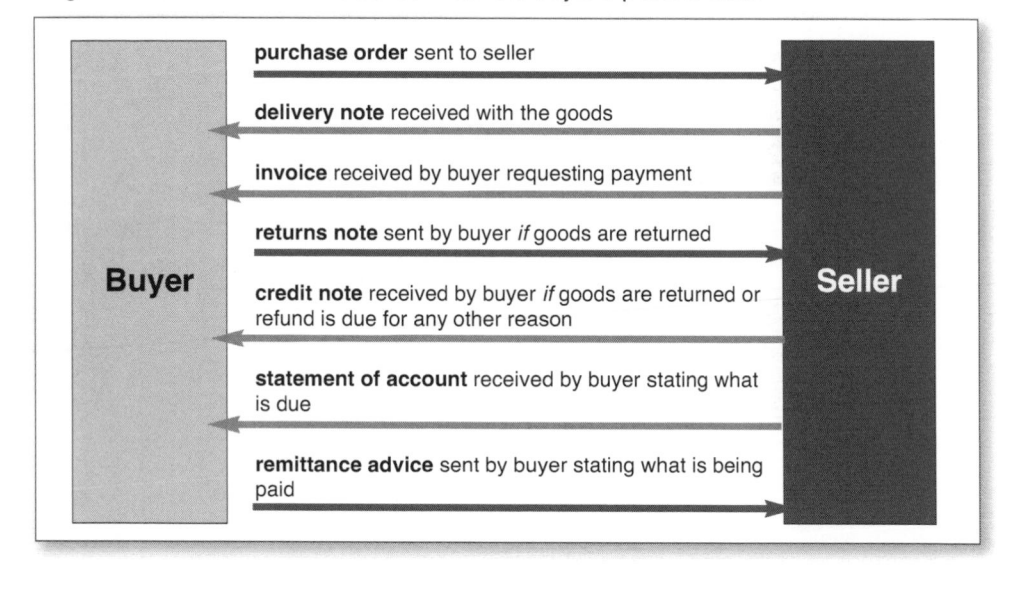

the invoice – setting out the payment due

Not all invoices are set out in exactly the same way, but they will all normally contain the same information. The details to be entered are indicated below.

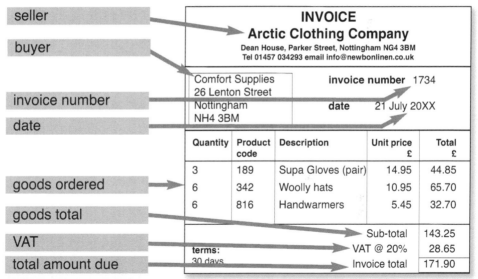

seller

buyer

invoice number

date

goods ordered

goods total

VAT

total amount due

INVOICE
Arctic Clothing Company
Dean House, Parker Street, Nottingham NG4 3BM
Tel 01457 034293 email info@newbonlinen.co.uk

Comfort Supplies
26 Lenton Street
Nottingham
NH4 3BM

invoice number 1734

date 21 July 20XX

Quantity	Product code	Description	Unit price £	Total £
3	189	Supa Gloves (pair)	14.95	44.85
6	342	Woolly hats	10.95	65.70
6	816	Handwarmers	5.45	32.70
			Sub-total	143.25
			VAT @ 20%	28.65
			Invoice total	171.90

terms:
30 days

credit note – setting out a reduction in the amount due

Credit notes are 'refund' documents set out in a very similar format to the invoice. They indicate to the buyer the reduction that will be made to the amount owing.

seller	
buyer	
credit note number	
date	
details of faulty goods returned	
reason for return	
total refund due, with VAT shown	

CREDIT NOTE
Arctic Clothing Company
Dean House, Parker Street, Nottingham NG4 3BM
Tel 01457 034293 email info@newbonlinen.co.uk

Comfort Supplies
26 Lenton Street
Nottingham
NH4 3BM

credit note number 634

date 31 July 20XX

Quantity	Product code	Description	Unit price £	Total £
1	612	Sheepskin hat	24.00	24.00

reason for return:
faulty goods

Sub-total	24.00
VAT @ 20%	4.80
Credit note total	28.80

statement of account – showing the amount due and for what

A statement of account is sent out to a customer who buys on credit, setting out:

- details of entries to the customer account (with appropriate reference numbers)
- amounts invoiced (debit column)
- payments received and credit notes received (credit column)
- a running total of the account (balance column) including the total amount owed

STATEMENT OF ACCOUNT			FROM **Vogue Limited**	
TO Ditzy Dames 67 Martley Road Borchester BO1 9BC			56 Shaftesbury Road Manorfield MA1 6GP	
date	**details**	**debit (£)**	**credit (£)**	**balance (£)**
01 03 20XX	Balance b/f	250.00		250.00
02 03 20XX	Payment received		220.00	30.00
02 03 20XX	Invoice 78254	890.50		920.50
10 03 20XX	Credit note 12157		44.00	876.50
			TOTAL	**876.50**

remittance advice – notification of a payment made and what it covers

A remittance advice is sent to the seller by a credit customer, indicating what is being paid in settlement of an account and **how**. The remittance advice sets out:

■ the date, amount and invoice number for invoices included in the payment

■ the date, amount and credit note number for credit notes deducted from the payment (the amount may be shown in brackets as it is a 'minus' amount)

■ the total payment amount and the means of payment, eg 'cheque' or 'BACS'

REMITTANCE ADVICE

TO

Molto di Moda
45 Floral Street
London N19 6GH

9 July 20XX

FROM

Vogue Limited
56 Shaftesbury Road
Manorfield
MA1 6GP

date	your reference	our reference	payment amount
03 06 XX	INVOICE 787213	876225	460.00
15 06 XX	CREDIT NOTE 12088	876225	(92.00)
	BACS PAYMENT TOTAL		368.00

a note on coding

Coding means giving something a unique series of letters and/or numbers which will identify that 'something'. Common examples are car registration plates, postcodes, National Insurance numbers, flight numbers, online catalogue numbers.

In a business context unique codes are used to identify documents such as purchases orders, invoices, credit notes and stock items.

There are various systems of coding which can be used:

- ■ **alphabetical** – using just letters, eg 'ABC'
- ■ **numeric** – using just numbers, normally in sequence, eg '217845'
- ■ **alpha-numeric** – using letters and numbers, eg 'FAB1236'

Common examples of coding in accounting include:

- ■ **numeric** – invoice and credit note numbers, ledger account numbers
- ■ **alpha-numeric** – stock codes, credit customer account codes (which can start with the first letters of the customer name), eg 'CAM207'

Checking of coding is essential when documents need to 'match up' in the accounting system, eg an order reference with an invoice and statement.

THE INVOICE – THE NEED FOR ACCURATE DETAILS

There is no 'right' or 'wrong' format for an invoice, but there must be certain basic details given which will enable the correct calculation to take place. These are shown in the format on the next page.

These details include:

- **quantity** – the number of items (taken from the purchase order)

- **code** – the stock or catalogue code of the product (taken from the purchase order)

- **description** – what the product is, eg a computer, an hour charged for book-keeping services

- **amount** – the total price before VAT is added on and after the deduction of discount (the 'net' price)

- **VAT** – the amount charged for VAT (sales tax)

- **total** – the price after VAT (sales tax) has been added on (the 'gross' amount)

an invoice calculation

This example is just one way in which the calculations on an invoice or credit note may be set out. You will encounter many different formats in practice. The important point is that all the details listed on the previous page must be present in one form or another so that the calculations can be seen and checked.

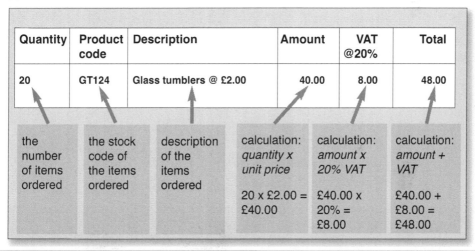

Quantity	Product code	Description	Amount	VAT @20%	Total
20	GT124	Glass tumblers @ £2.00	40.00	8.00	48.00

the number of items ordered

the stock code of the items ordered

description of the items ordered

calculation: *quantity x unit price*

20 x £2.00 = £40.00

calculation: *amount x 20% VAT*

£40.00 x 20% = £8.00

calculation: *amount + VAT*

£40.00 + £8.00 = £48.00

7 Discounts and VAT

CALCULATING DISCOUNTS

Calculating discounts can sometimes be a problem. Calculating settlement (cash) discount is very often a problem.

But, as with many problem areas in accounting, discounts can be sorted out by remembering a series of defined steps.

You will first need to remember the types of discount:

- **Trade discount** – a percentage reduction in the selling price given by sellers to established customers, normally businesses (ie 'in the trade') rather than the general public.

- **Bulk discount** – a percentage reduction in the selling price given by sellers to customers who buy large quantities; the percentage sometimes increases in line with the quantity supplied.

These two types of discount are shown on invoices and credit notes but **not in the accounting records**.

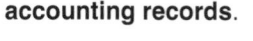

■ **Settlement discount** – also known as **cash discount** is a reduction in the selling price of goods which can be deducted by the customer when payment is made promptly, eg 'within 7 days.'

This discount is **optional**, and is **recorded in the accounting records** as an expense to the seller.

calculation of trade and bulk discount

Trade and **bulk** discount are more straightforward. They are a standard percentage deduction from the selling price, as shown below and illustrated on the next page.

EXAMPLE

Here 100 glass tumblers which cost £2 each before discount or VAT are sold with a 20% trade discount given to the buyer. The calculation is:

1	Calculate the price **before** discount	100 x £2	=	£200
2	Calculate the **20%** trade discount on £200	£200 x $\frac{20}{100}$	=	£40
3	Calculate the price **after** deducting discount	£200 – £40	=	£160

Quantity	Product code	Description	Amount	VAT @20%	Total
100	GT124	Glass tumblers @ £2.00	160.00	32.00	192.00

calculation: 100 x £2.00 = £200.00 minus 20% discount (£40) = £160. Note that the deduction of the £40 is not shown on the invoice, just the net total of £160. The VAT calculation is explained on the next page.

- The price after the deduction of discount is known as the **net price** and is shown on the extract from the invoice above in the column heading 'Amount.'

- The 'Amount' column is also sometimes shown with the heading '**Net**'.

- The actual amount of the trade discount is not shown on the above invoice, although some invoices show the price before and after discount is deducted.

calculation of VAT (sales tax)

A **sales tax** – **VAT** (Value Added Tax in the UK) – is normally **added** to the net total on an invoice or credit note after any trade or bulk discount has been deducted. In the example below the tax is calculated as 20% of the amount.

EXAMPLE

This continues the calculation on the invoice shown on the previous page.

1	Calculate the **20%** VAT on the £160 total and enter the figure in the VAT column	£160 x $\frac{20}{100}$ = £32
2	Add the **£32 VAT to** the £160 and enter the £192 in the Total column	£160 + **£32** = £192

The customer will be charged £192. The invoice calculation will look like this:

Quantity	Product code	Description	Amount	VAT @20%	Total
100	GT124	Glass tumblers @ £2.00	160.00	32.00	192.00

settlement (cash) discount – problems?

Settlement (cash) discount is an optional discount which can be deducted by the customer when payment is made promptly, eg 'within 7 days'.

The calculation of settlement discount does sometimes cause problems. The rules are shown below, and an example follows.

the rules of settlement discount

- the discount is **optional** – it is not deducted if payment is made **later** than the earlier date given

- the 'Amount' box on the invoice **always** shows the amount charged **before** any deduction of settlement discount

- the **reduced amount** after deduction of settlement discount is **not normally shown on the invoice**

- settlement discount is deducted from the amount charged **after the deduction of trade or bulk discount** and **before the addition of VAT,** ie from the 'net' amount in the 'Amount' box

- ■ BUT . . . the **VAT** is always calculated on the amount **after the deduction of settlement (cash) discount, whether it is taken or not** and this is the amount shown in the VAT box

- ■ AND SO . . . the final Total box is always the result of the following calculation (and this seems illogical and can cause confusion)

  Total = the amount charged for the goods **before** the deduction of settlement discount

  plus VAT calculated on the amount **after** the deduction of settlement discount

- ■ AND SO . . . the amount paid by the customer will **always include the reduced VAT amount** plus the total goods amount either with settlement discount deducted for early payment or the full amount if the invoice is paid later than the early payment date.

  Simple!

  Now follow the example on the next few pages.

EXAMPLE

This example carries on the example given earlier: 100 glass tumblers costing £2 each are sold with a 20% trade discount given to the buyer.

In addition, 5% settlement discount is offered to the buyer for settlement within seven days. The buyer decides to take the settlement discount.

The calculation is shown below, after the deduction of the 20% trade discount of £40 which produces a net total of £200 – £40 = £160. This figure goes in the Amount column.

1 NOW calculate the 5% settlement discount.   £160 x 5/100   =   £8

2 Calculate the reduced amount payable before   £160 – £8   =   £152
   VAT by deducting the settlement discount from
   the £160. This figure is not normally written
   on the invoice.

3 Calculate VAT @ 20% on this reduced amount   £152 x 20%   =   £30.40
   (this **is** written on the invoice in the VAT box).

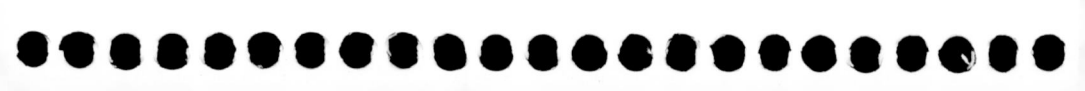

4   Calculate the total invoice charge using the   £160 + £30.40 = £190.40
figures written on the invoice (ie the goods total
before settlement discount is deducted).

The calculation section of the 5% settlement discount invoice will look like this:

Quantity	Product code	Description	Amount	VAT @20%	Total
100	GT124	Glass tumblers @ £2.00	160.00	30.40	190.40

VAT is calculated on
the total amount *less*
the 5% settlement
discount, ie £152

£152 x
20% =
£30.40

£160 +
£30.40
= £190.40

settlement discount – points to remember

The figures that go on the invoice are:

- the **higher** total in the Amount box (this is the figure **before** deduction of settlement discount)

- the **lower** VAT amount in the VAT box (this is the figure based on the goods amount **after** deduction of settlement discount)

Quantity	Product code	Description	Amount	VAT @20%	Total
100	GT124	Glass tumblers @ £2.00	160.00	30.40	190.40

In this example the customer will pay:

- if settlement discount **is taken**, the lower goods total of £152.00 (not shown on invoice) plus the lower VAT amount (shown) of £30.40, making a payment total of £182.40 (not shown on invoice)

- if discount **is not taken** - the higher goods amount of £160.00 (shown) and the lower VAT amount (shown) of £30.40, making a payment total of £190.40 (shown)

some notes on VAT and rounding

formula for working out the VAT on a given (net) amount

$$\text{amount} \times \frac{\text{VAT rate}}{100} = \text{VAT to be charged}$$

example: $£120 \times \dfrac{20}{100} = £24$ (to be added on to the £120 = £144)

calculating the VAT at a given rate included in a whole (gross) amount (eg £144)

- **Method 1** (VAT fraction of $^1/_6$*): if VAT is 20%, divide the whole amount by 6.
  example: £144 ÷ 6 = VAT of £24

  * the VAT fraction is published by HMRC at www.HMRC.gov.uk

- **Method 2** (which is far more complicated):
  $$\frac{\text{VAT percentage (20)} \times \text{whole amount including VAT (£144)}}{100 + \text{VAT percentage (ie 100 + 20)}} = \text{VAT of £24}$$

'rounding' in calculations

- with **normal** calculations you should round **up or down** to the nearest figure
- when calculating **VAT** you should **normally** round **down** to the nearest figure
- use the number of decimal places specified (it is often two decimal places)

basic accounting 1 wise guide – discounts and VAT

8 Documents to day books

DAY BOOKS AND THE ACCOUNTING SYSTEM – AN OVERVIEW

The day books are summaries of financial transactions and form a vital link between financial documents (invoices and credit notes) and the double-entry ledger accounts.

what is a day book?

A day book is a **summary list of financial transactions, compiled from invoices or credit notes**. It enables a business to transfer a summary of sales and purchases transactions to the double-entry ledger accounts from a whole 'day' (or other set period) rather than one-by-one, which could prove complicated and time-consuming.

Day books are known as books of **prime entry**. As well as day books there are other books of prime entry in the accounting system including **cash book** and **petty cash book**. As with the day books, these books of prime entry are used as a 'first stop' summary to record financial transactions which are then entered in the accounts.

sales and purchases day books

Sales and purchases day books summarise information extracted from:

■ invoices and credit notes issued to customers – **sales documents**

■ invoices and credit notes received from suppliers – **purchases documents**

There are four day books:

sales day book	compiled from **sales invoices** (invoices issued to customers)
sales returns day book	compiled from **sales credit notes** (issued to customers)
purchases day book	compiled from **purchases invoices** (invoices issued by suppliers)
purchases returns day book	compiled from **purchases credit notes** (issued by suppliers)

The next page shows how these day books fit into the accounting system.

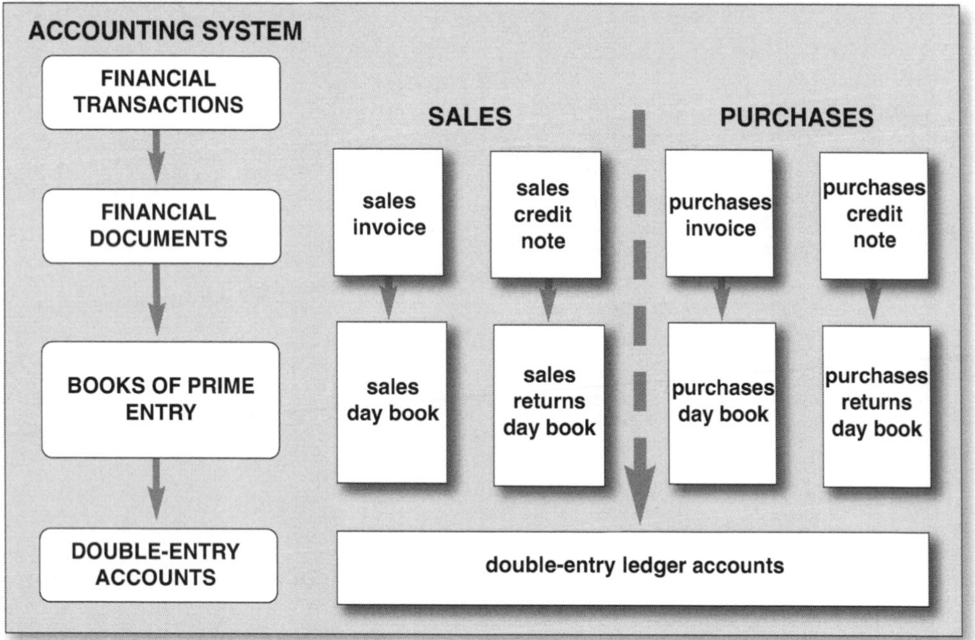

ACCOUNTING SYSTEM

FINANCIAL TRANSACTIONS

↓

FINANCIAL DOCUMENTS

↓

BOOKS OF PRIME ENTRY

↓

DOUBLE-ENTRY ACCOUNTS

SALES

PURCHASES

sales invoice	sales credit note		purchases invoice	purchases credit note
↓	↓		↓	↓
sales day book	sales returns day book		purchases day book	purchases returns day book

double-entry ledger accounts

format of day books

There is no set format for day books. The example format shown below is commonly used. The details entered in the various columns are taken from each individual sales invoice. The same procedure is followed for the other three day books using the appropriate invoice or credit note.

EXAMPLE: SALES DAY BOOK

Date 20XX	Details	Invoice Number	Total	VAT	Net
5 Aug	AB Supplies	19381	96.00	16.00	80.00
6 Aug	S Gerrard Limited	19382	144.00	24.00	120.00
7 Aug	Hermes Sports	19383	240.00	40.00	200.00

| the date of the invoice issued | the name of the customer | the invoice number | the invoice total **after** VAT has been added on | the VAT total from the invoice | the invoice total **before** VAT has been added on |

totalling the day books

The money columns of each day book must be totalled from time-to-time and it is these totals that will be transferred to various double-entry accounts in the appropriate ledgers. The totalling process is explained in the boxes below.

EXAMPLE: TOTALLED SALES DAY BOOK

Date 20XX	Details	Invoice Number	Total	VAT	Net
5 Aug	AB Supplies	19381	96.00	16.00	80.00
6 Aug	S Gerrard Limited	19382	144.00	24.00	120.00
7 Aug	Hermes Sports	19383	240.00	40.00	200.00
8 Aug			480.00	80.00	400.00

enter the date on which the day book is totalled

The 'Total', 'VAT' and 'Net' columns are all totalled.
The arithmetic is checked by adding the 'Net' and 'VAT' column totals. The result should equal the 'Total' column. In this case:
£400 + £80 = £480

NEXT STEP – WRITING UP THE LEDGER ACCOUNTS

After the day books have been completed, the next step is the periodic transfer of the day book entries to the double-entry ledger accounts.

*We will first deal with the **sales day book** and the **sales returns day book**.*

which ledgers?

The two ledgers that will be used are the **sales ledger** and the **general ledger.**

On the next two pages you can see how the figures are transferred to the accounts.

SALES LEDGER	GENERAL LEDGER

◼ individual **personal customer accounts** showing entries for
  - credit sales
  - credit sales returns
	◼ **sales ledger control account** (total of credit customer accounts)
	◼ **sales account** (total of sales)
	◼ **sales returns account** (total of returns)
	◼ **VAT account** (VAT received)

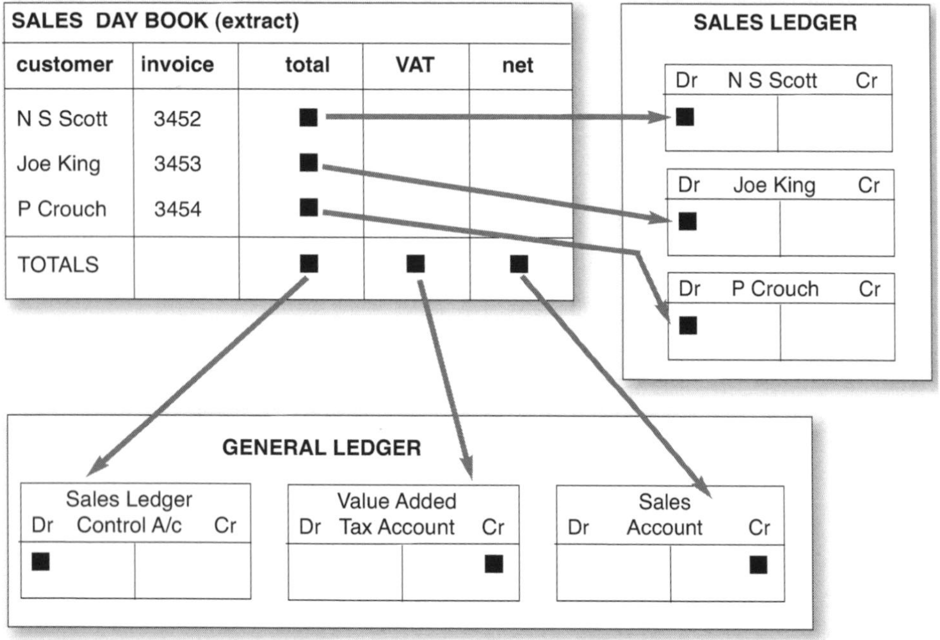

SALES DAY BOOK (extract)

customer	invoice	total	VAT	net
N S Scott	3452	■		
Joe King	3453	■		
P Crouch	3454	■		
TOTALS		■	■	■

SALES LEDGER

Dr	N S Scott	Cr
■		

Dr	Joe King	Cr
■		

Dr	P Crouch	Cr
■		

GENERAL LEDGER

	Sales Ledger	
Dr	Control A/c	Cr
■		

	Value Added	
Dr	Tax Account	Cr
		■

	Sales	
Dr	Account	Cr
		■

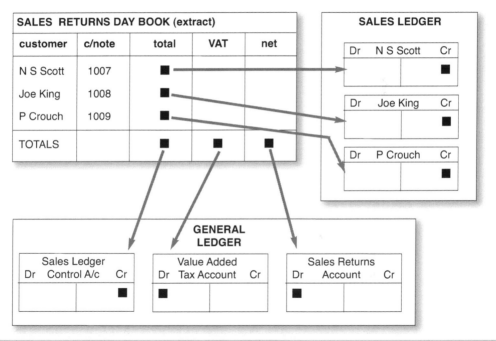

SALES RETURNS DAY BOOK (extract)				
customer	**c/note**	**total**	**VAT**	**net**
N S Scott	1007	■		
Joe King	1008	■		
P Crouch	1009	■		
TOTALS		■	■	■

SALES LEDGER

Dr	N S Scott	Cr
		■

Dr	Joe King	Cr
		■

Dr	P Crouch	Cr
		■

GENERAL LEDGER

Sales Ledger	
Dr Control A/c	Cr
	■

Value Added	
Dr Tax Account	Cr
■	

Sales Returns	
Dr Account	Cr
■	

PURCHASES: FROM DAY BOOKS TO DOUBLE-ENTRY ACCOUNTS

*Transfer of figures from the **purchases day book** and the **purchases returns day book** work in the same way as the transfers from the sales day books, except that supplier accounts relating to credit purchases are contained in the **purchases ledger**.*

which ledgers?

The ledgers that will be used are the **purchases ledger** and the **general ledger.**

On the next two pages you can see how the figures are transferred to the accounts.

PURCHASES LEDGER	GENERAL LEDGER

▪ individual **personal supplier accounts** showing entries for
  - credit purchases
  - credit purchases returns
	▪ **purchases ledger control account** (total of credit supplier accounts)
	▪ **purchases account** (total purchases)
	▪ **purchases returns account** (total returns)
	▪ **VAT account** (VAT paid)

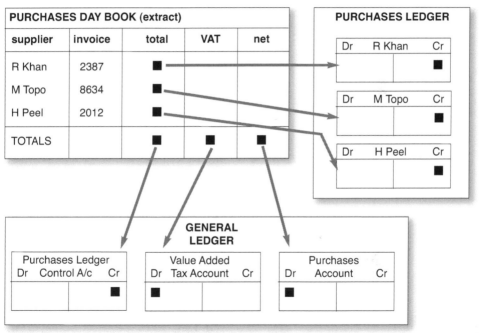

PURCHASES DAY BOOK (extract)				
supplier	invoice	total	VAT	net
R Khan	2387	■		
M Topo	8634	■		
H Peel	2012	■		
TOTALS		■	■	■

PURCHASES LEDGER

Dr	R Khan	Cr
		■

Dr	M Topo	Cr
		■

Dr	H Peel	Cr
		■

GENERAL LEDGER

Purchases Ledger	
Dr Control A/c	Cr
	■

Value Added	
Dr Tax Account	Cr
■	

Purchases	
Dr Account	Cr
■	

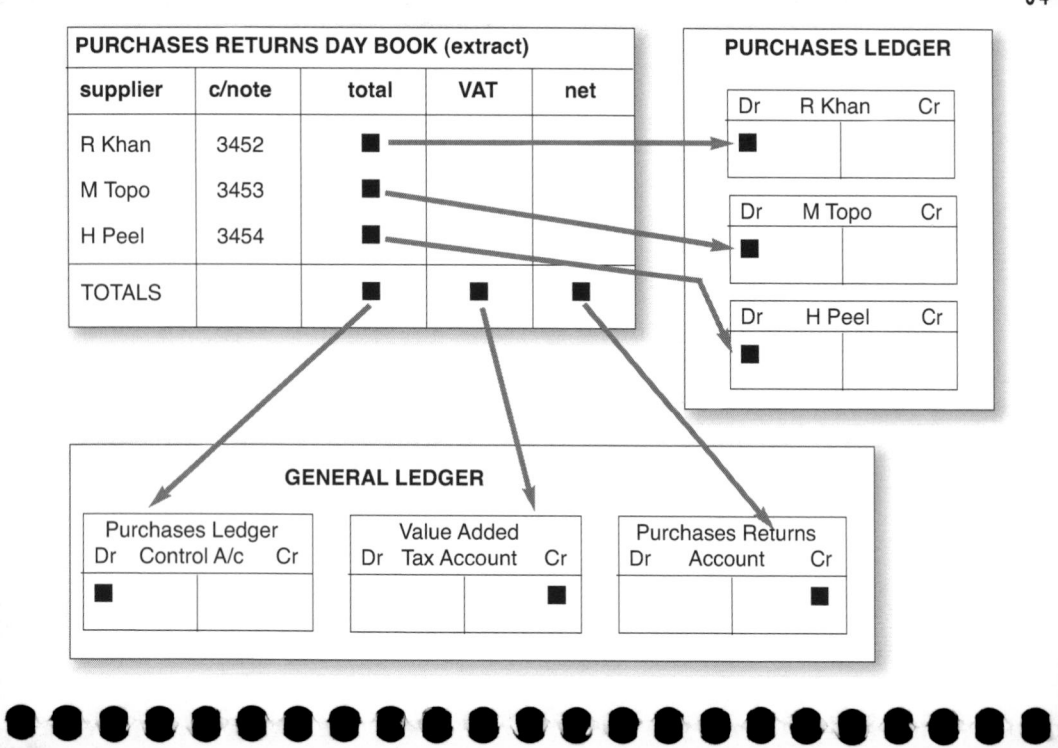

CASH BOOK – A BOOK OF PRIME ENTRY

*Books of prime entry – the day books, for example – are the first place in the accounting system where financial data is recorded. The **cash book** is an important book of prime entry and a source of data for posting to the double-entry ledger accounts.*

The **cash book** incorporates two double-entry accounts which record:
- cash (notes and coins) received and paid out – this is **cash account**
- incoming bank payments and outgoing bank payments – this is **bank account**

■ The cash book records
- **money in** on **the left** – these are **debits**
- **money out** on **the right** – these are **credits**

debit (dr)	CASH BOOK	credit (cr)
Money in		**Money out**

how to work out the debits and credits for cash book transactions

◼ If the transaction is a **receipt** (money in), the entry in the cash book will be a **debit** and so **the other entry will be a credit,** for example to the account of a customer who has paid an invoice, or for cash received from cash sales.

◼ If the transaction is a **payment** (money out), the entry in the cash book will be a **credit** and so **the other entry will be a debit**, for example to the account of a supplier who has been sent a payment, or cash used to pay for expenses.

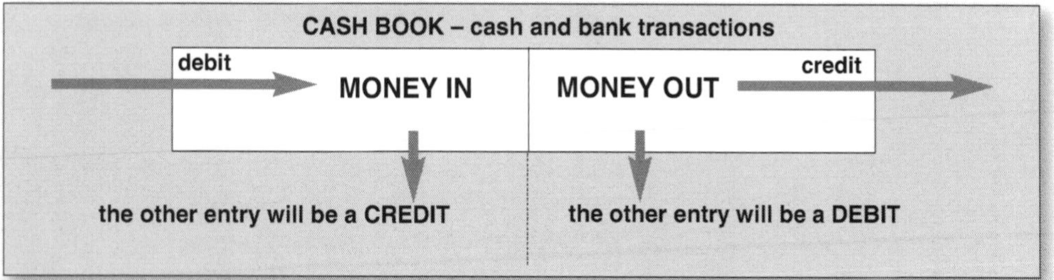

CASH BOOK – cash and bank transactions	
debit → **MONEY IN**	**MONEY OUT** credit →
⬇	⬇
the other entry will be a CREDIT	the other entry will be a DEBIT

*If you need further help with **debits and credits** in double-entry, please see pages 11-13.*

the cash book – format

There are a number of different ways in which a cash book may be set up.

These different formats will depend on the type and size of organisation which uses the cash book. The typical traditional cash book shown below contains:

- debit and credit sides – like a double entry 'T' account

- bank account columns and cash account columns

- columns for VAT

- columns for settlement discount (allowed and received)

Dr					**CASH BOOK**				Cr
Date	Details	Discount allowed	VAT	Bank	Date	Details	Discount received	VAT	Bank

what goes through the cash book, and on what side?

Money received is entered on the **left (debit) side** and **payments out** on the **right (credit) side**. All these items are then written up in the various ledgers.

The diagram below shows the different types of payment, and the debit and credit entries made in a cash book with bank and cash columns.

Dr					**CASH BOOK**						Cr
Date	Details	Discount allowed	VAT	Cash	Bank	Date	Details	Discount received	VAT	Cash	Bank

receipts (debits)
- cash receipts from cash customers
- bank receipts from credit customers
- loans received into the bank account
- transfers from other bank accounts
- money paid in by the owners (capital)

payments out (credits)
- payments to suppliers
- payments for expenses
- loan repayments
- transfers to other bank accounts
- payments for capital items (eg a car)
- drawings (money taken out by the owners)

double-entry from the cash book receipts (left-hand) side

The diagram below shows examples of the **credit** account entries which are made to complete the double-entry from the **debit** side of the cash book.

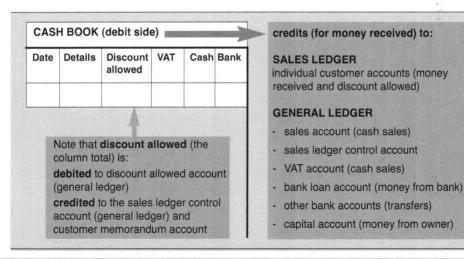

CASH BOOK (debit side)

Date	Details	Discount allowed	VAT	Cash	Bank

Note that **discount allowed** (the column total) is:

debited to discount allowed account (general ledger)

credited to the sales ledger control account (general ledger) and customer memorandum account

credits (for money received) to:

SALES LEDGER
individual customer accounts (money received and discount allowed)

GENERAL LEDGER
- sales account (cash sales)
- sales ledger control account
- VAT account (cash sales)
- bank loan account (money from bank)
- other bank accounts (transfers)
- capital account (money from owner)

double-entry from the cash book payments (right-hand) side

The diagram below shows examples of the **debit** account entries which are made to complete the double-entry from the **credit** side of the cash book.

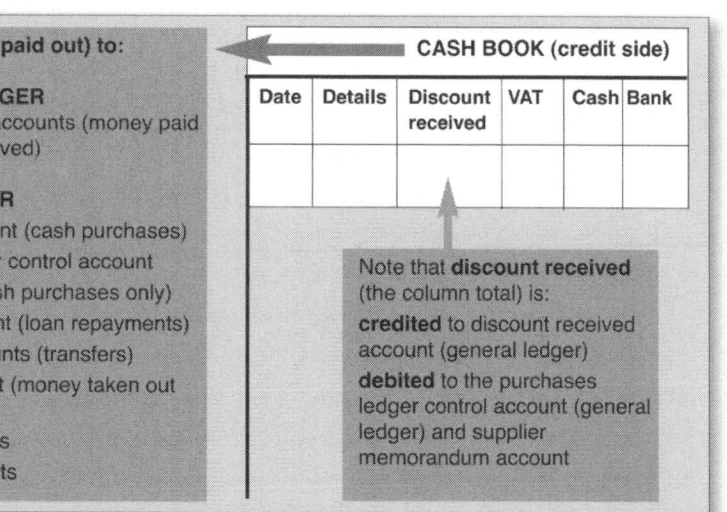

debits (for money paid out) to:

PURCHASES LEDGER
individual supplier accounts (money paid and discounts received)

GENERAL LEDGER
- purchases account (cash purchases)
- purchases ledger control account
- VAT account (cash purchases only)
- bank loan account (loan repayments)
- other bank accounts (transfers)
- drawings account (money taken out by the owners)
- expense accounts
- purchase of assets

CASH BOOK (credit side)

Date	Details	Discount received	VAT	Cash	Bank

Note that **discount received** (the column total) is:

credited to discount received account (general ledger)

debited to the purchases ledger control account (general ledger) and supplier memorandum account

cash book – points to watch out for

▨ **Is the bank or cash account contained in the cash book?**

In this Wise Guide the bank or cash accounts shown in the cash book are the actual **double-entry accounts** belonging to the general ledger. In this case these accounts do not need posting to the ledgers.

Sometimes the bank or cash accounts contained in the cash book are not double-entry accounts and need to be posted to **separate bank or cash control accounts in the general ledger**. In this case the cash book is used only as a **book of prime entry**.

▨ **Cash transactions only in the VAT columns**

Remember that the entries in the VAT columns relate to cash sales or purchases only. These are posted to the VAT account from the cash book.

VAT on credit sales and credit purchases **has already been posted to the ledger accounts through the day books.**

▨ **The use of analysis columns**

There are many different cash book formats. Another format that you might come across will have analysis columns for different types of expense.

Petty cash book - how it fits into the accounting system

*A **petty cash book** records small cash payments for purchases and expenses, eg stationery, postage and taxi fares.*

*A petty cash book can also be a book of **prime entry** and a source of data for posting to the double-entry ledger accounts.*

the petty cash procedure

■ **petty cash** is a small store of notes and coins – up to £100 for example – kept in a locked tin and looked after by the **petty cashier**

■ someone making a small cash purchase fills in a **petty cash voucher** with the details of the purchase and attaches the receipt to the petty cash voucher

■ the petty cashier checks all the details, authorises the voucher and gives the person the cash from the petty cash box – they both sign the voucher

■ the relevant details on the petty cash voucher are then recorded by the petty cashier in a **petty cash book** - see the next page for a typical voucher

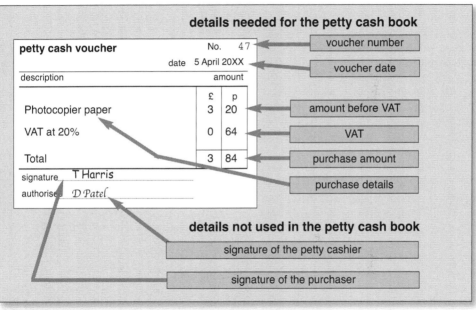

petty cash voucher	No. 47			voucher number
	date 5 April 20XX			voucher date
description	amount			
	£	p		
Photocopier paper	3	20		amount before VAT
VAT at 20%	0	64		VAT
Total	3	84		purchase amount
signature T Harris				purchase details
authorised D Patel				

details needed for the petty cash book

details not used in the petty cash book

signature of the petty cashier

signature of the purchaser

The format of the petty cash book is shown on the next page.

PETTY CASH BOOK LAYOUT

Cash receipts 'in' (debit side)				Cash payments 'out' (credit side) - with analysis columns					
Date 20XX	Details	Voucher Number	Amount	Date 20XX	Details	Amount	VAT	Postage	Office expenses
30 Jun	Opening Balance		100.00						
		52		1 Jul	Postage stamps	26.00		26.00	
		53		4 Jul	Coffee & tea	14.40	2.40		12.00
		54		5 Jul	Thick bleach	3.60	0.60		3.00
				5 Jul	Copy paper	24.00	4.00		20.00
						68.00	7.00	26.00	35.00

petty cash voucher numbers

cash received into petty cash tin

the transaction dates

the total amounts from the petty cash vouchers

the VAT amounts from the petty cash vouchers

column totals

analysed expense amounts with VAT deducted

petty cash book – recording transactions

The petty cash book:

■ has a **debit** side for **cash paid in** when the petty cash tin is topped up

■ has a **credit** side for **cash paid out**

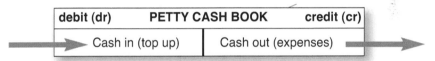

debit (dr)	PETTY CASH BOOK	credit (cr)
Cash in (top up)	Cash out (expenses)	

■ the **credit side** records the details from the petty cash vouchers:

- the date and the **total** amount of each voucher

- the details of what has been bought, eg postage stamps, cleaning materials

- the VAT content of the voucher

- the **'net'** amount of the voucher (before VAT) in the correct analysis column, eg 'Postage', Office expenses, Stationery, Fuel etc . . .

■ the Amount, VAT and analysis columns are then all added up

■ all the totals are checked by 'cross casting' – as you would in a day book; here the calculation is £7.00 + £26.00 + £35.00 = £68.00

petty cash book – its place in the accounting system

The petty cash book can be **a book of prime entry**:

■ it is the main source from which details are taken to make entries in the ledgers

■ in this case the general ledger will include a **petty cash control account** to summarise payments in and out of petty cash

Note: the petty cash book can sometimes incorporate the double-entry petty cash account (General Ledger), but in this example it is purely a book of prime entry.

Using the petty cash book shown on the next page, the double-entry postings are:

■ **receipt of cash**	**debit**	Petty cash control account	£100.00	
	credit	Bank account	£100.00	
■ **petty cash payments**	using the credit side **totals** as follows:			
	debit	VAT account		£7.00
	debit	Postage account		£26.00
	debit	Office expenses account		£35.00
				£68.00
and then . . .				
	credit	Petty cash control account		£68.00

PETTY CASH BOOK LAYOUT (used as a book of prime entry)

	Cash receipts 'in' (debit side)				Cash payments 'out' (credit side) - with analysis columns				
Date 20XX	Details	Voucher Number	Amount	Date 20XX	Details	Amount	VAT	Postage	Office expenses
30 Jun	Opening Balance		100.00						
		52		1 Jul	Postage stamps	26.00		26.00	
		53		4 Jul	Coffee & tea	14.40	2.40		12.00
		54		5 Jul	Thick bleach	3.60	0.60		3.00
				5 Jul	Copy paper	24.00	4.00		20.00
						68.00	7.00	26.00	35.00

GENERAL LEDGER
Note: as this £100 is an **opening balance**, 'top ups' of cash will have taken place before 30 June.
In each case the entries will have been:
debit petty cash control account
credit bank account

GENERAL LEDGER
credit petty cash control account £68.00

GENERAL LEDGER
debit VAT account £7.00

GENERAL LEDGER
debit Postage account £26.00

GENERAL LEDGER
debit Office Expenses account £35.00

13 Balancing accounts

WHY DO ACCOUNTS NEED BALANCING?

*Balancing an account means calculating the **up-to-date total amount** in any account at the end of a period, eg total sales, the bank balance, the total wages paid out. These figures are needed for **management** and also for setting up the **trial balance**.*

steps for calculating an account balance

Look at the customer account below and follow the numbered steps on the pages that follow to find out the customer's balance, ie how much Bella Catering owes.

Dr			Bella Catering		Cr
		£			£
1 Mar	Balance b/d	200	3 Mar	Bank	200
4 Mar	Sales	250	15 Mar	Sales returns	50
5 Mar	Sales	300			

Step 1 – total the debit and credit columns and work out the difference

▓ Add up the debit and credit columns to produce separate totals.

▓ Do not enter figures in ink in the account at this stage.

▓ You can write down the totals on a separate piece of paper – or pencil in the figures in the account as a temporary subtotal, as shown in grey here.

▓ Work out the difference between the two totals. This is the **balance**, the amount owed by Bella Catering. The calculation is: £750 – £250 = **£500**

You will need this total for the next step when you write this balance in the account.

Dr		£		Bella Catering	Cr £
1 Mar	Balance b/d	200	3 Mar	Bank	200
4 Mar	Sales	250	15 Mar	Sales returns	50
5 Mar	Sales	300		temporary totals can be pencilled in	
		750			*250*

Step 2 – enter the balance on the correct side and calculate the column totals

■ Enter the balance you have worked out in Step 1 (£500)

  - on the side of the lower total (here it is the credit side)

  - on the next available line (rubbing out any pencilled subtotals first)

  - plus the date and the description 'Balance c/d' (or 'Balance carried down')

■ Now total the debits and credits (the totals should be the same, in this case £750) and enter these totals on the same level. Put a single line above the totals and a double line or heavy line under the totals – this line means that nothing should be added or subtracted from these figures.

Dr		**Bella Catering**				Cr
		£			*enter the balance you have calculated*	£
1 Mar	Balance b/d	200	3 Mar	Bank		200
4 Mar	Sales	250	5 Mar	Sales returns		50
5 Mar	Sales	300	**5 Mar**	**Balance c/d**		**500**
	total up both columns and check the totals are the same	750				750

Step 3 – complete the double entry by carrying down the balance

▩ Because you have entered £500 on the **credit** side of this double-entry account you will also need to enter £500 on the **debit** side, but in the same account.

▩ This entry is made on the debit side on the next line **below** the totals of £750

- with the date of the next working day

- with the description of 'Balance b/d' (or 'Balance brought down').

Remember!

'**C**arried down' or '**c**/d' is always the entry higher up, beginning with 'c' = **c**rown

'**B**rought down' or '**b**/d' is always the entry below, beginning with 'b' = **b**ottom

Dr			**Bella Catering**				Cr
		£					£
1 Mar	Balance b/d	200		3 Mar	Bank		200
4 Mar	Sales	250		5 Mar	Sales returns		50
5 Mar	Sales	300		**5 Mar**	**Balance c/d**		**500**
		750					750
6 Mar	**Balance b/d**	**500**					

the balance b/d is normally a day after the balance c/d

enter the balance you have calculated

14 Account reconciliation

WHY DO ACCOUNTS NEED RECONCILING?

If you order goods from a supplier on a regular basis on credit you will receive a statement, often monthly, stating what they have invoiced and what you have paid and listing any returns and credit notes issued.

What if their statement and your account do not agree? You should always reconcile ('match up') the items on the supplier statement against the entries in the supplier account in your purchases ledger.

what could cause a difference between the account and the statement?

- you have made payment but it does not yet show on the statement
- a wrong amount is entered on the account or on the statement
- an invoice or credit note shows on the statement but you have not received it
- an invoice shows on the statement but you are disputing it, possibly because the goods sent are faulty or you have been overcharged by the supplier who does not agree with your complaint

how to reconcile the difference – reconciliation statement

- make sure the supplier's account in the purchases ledger has been balanced
- tick off the items that are both in the supplier statement and the supplier's account in the purchases ledger
- if there is any item that is not ticked in either the statement or the account, this should account for the difference between the final balance of the statement and the balance brought down of the supplier's account
- complete a Reconciliation Statement, showing the difference and the reason for the difference (eg payment from you not received by the supplier, or an invoice/credit note not received by you from the supplier) – see below:

RECONCILIATION STATEMENT	
Balance on supplier statement	£512.60
Balance on supplier account in purchases ledger	£361.20
Difference	£151.40
Reason for difference: Payment for £151.40 not yet received by supplier	

EXAMPLE

reconciling the statement with the supplier account in the purchases ledger

SUPPLIER STATEMENT: BAXO IMPORTERS (extract)				
date	details	debit (£)	credit (£)	balance (£)
1 Nov 20XX	Balance b/d			✔ 650.00
5 Nov 20XX	BACS payment		✔ 650.00	00.00
19 Nov 20XX	Invoice 1902	✔ 850.00		850.00
26 Nov 20XX	Credit note 534		85.00	765.00
30 Nov 20XX	Total			765.00

item not in the supplier account

Dr	PURCHASES LEDGER: Baxo Importers					Cr
20XX		£	20XX			£
8 Nov	Bank	✔650.00	1 Nov	Balance b/d		✔ 650.00
30 Nov	Balance c/d	850.00	22 Nov	Purchases (Inv. 1902)		✔ 850.00
		1500.00				1500.00
			1 Dec	Balance b/d		850.00

drawing up the reconciliation statement

In the example shown on the previous page, note that:

- items in both the supplier statement and supplier account have been ticked off

- there is one item extra on the statement – a credit note for £85.00; this has not been ticked off

- this £85.00 represents the difference between the final balances of the supplier statement and the account, ie £85.00

- this is then recorded on the reconciliation statement shown below

---

RECONCILIATION STATEMENT

Balance on supplier statement	£765.00
Balance on supplier account in purchases ledger	£850.00
Difference	– £85.00

Reason for difference:
Credit note for £85.00 not yet received from supplier

---

reconciling payments from customers

A business that sells on credit should also make sure that payments received from customers reconcile (match up) with:

▇ the sales documents the business issues, eg invoices and credit notes

▇ previous payments received from the customer

A common practice is to reconcile each incoming payment against the details of the customer account in the sales ledger.

The two documents that are frequently compared are:

▇ the **remittance advice** (if it includes details of what the payment covers)

▇ the latest customer **statement of account** (which will show all the transactions on the sales ledger account)

If there is a difference between the amount due shown on the statement and the amount received, it should be calculated and traced to the relevant document(s).

A reconciliation between the remittance advice and statement of account is shown on the next page.

REMITTANCE ADVICE

TO		FROM
Cool Socks Limited Unit 45 Elgar Estate, Broadfield BR7 4ER	8 November 20XX	Vogue Limited 56 Shaftesbury Road Manorfield MA1 6GP

date	your reference	our reference	payment amount
03 10 XX	INVOICE 787923	876103	283.20
11 10 XX	CREDIT NOTE 12157	876103	28.32
		BACS PAYMENT TOTAL	254.88

STATEMENT OF ACCOUNT (extract)   account reconciliation

date	details	debit (£)	credit (£)	balance (£)
01 10 20XX	Balance b/f	150.00		150.00
02 10 20XX	Payment received		150.00	00.00
02 10 20XX	Invoice 787923	283.20		283.20
10 10 20XX	Credit note 12157		28.32	254.88
			TOTAL	**254.88**

15 The trial balance

HOW ACCURATE IS THE DOUBLE-ENTRY?

Accuracy is important in any accounting system and businesses will use a number of checking processes to avoid mistakes.

Double-entry always requires debits to equal credits. This can be checked by adding up all the debit balances and all the credit balances in the general ledger and **making sure the two totals are the same**.

This is known as the **trial balance**.

the trial balance

- ▨ lists all the general ledger account balances at a specific date (eg the last day in the month) in two columns and adds them both up

- ▨ the left-hand column contains the debit balances and the right-hand column contains the credit balances

- ▨ the two totals *should* agree

EXAMPLE: TRIAL BALANCE

In the example here, a simple trial balance for ABC Ltd is drawn up on 31 May from the account balances shown on the left.

Account name	Balance (£)	ABC LTD TRIAL BALANCE AS AT 31 MAY	
		Debit (£)	Credit (£)
Bank (cash at bank)	2,000	2,000	
Capital	20,000		20,000
Electricity	395	395	
Insurance	935	935	
Machinery	4,900	4,900	
Payables	2,700		2,700
Purchases	49,970	49,970	
Receivables	3,500	3,500	
Sales	81,000		81,000
VAT (payable to HMRC)	870		870
Wages	42,870	42,870	
		Total 104,570	104,570

debit or credit?

- In an exam situation you are likely to be given a list of balances but you will not be told whether each figure is a debit or a credit.

- The problem here, of course, is deciding between debit or credit.

- The rules are straightforward and can be remembered by the two words:

DEAD (for the **debits**)   **C**LIC (for the **credits**)

These words stand for the types of account listed in the trial balance:

D ebit balances	**C** redit balances
E xpenses	**L** iabilities
A ssets	**I** ncome
D rawings	**C** apital

'DEAD CLIC' is just one way of helping you to remember your debits and credits. Your tutor may suggest other ways. See the next Section (page 84) for making your own 'Memory aids'.

notes on DEAD CLIC

DEAD = debit balances

Debits are items that a business owns, money it is owed and money it pays out.

- **D**ebits

- **E**xpenses   Expenses of the business, eg purchases, wages, insurance.

- **A**ssets   Items owned by the business, eg money in bank, inventory, computers, property, receivables (amounts owed to the business).

- **D**rawings   Money or inventory taken out of a business by the owner(s).

CLIC = credit balances

Credits are items that a business owes and money it receives.

- **C**redits

- **L**iabilities   Items owed by the business, eg loans, bank overdraft, payables (money owed to suppliers).

- **I**ncome   Money coming into the business, eg sales, rent received.

- **C**apital   Money invested by the owner in the business.

trial balance – points to watch out for

Nothing is ever completely straightforward in accounting and there are **some accounts which can have either debit or credit balances.**

These need to be transferred to either the debit or the credit column of the trial balance as appropriate.

You will always be given information which will tell you whether the balance is debit or credit.

There are two main examples:

- **Bank account**   Money in the bank (sometimes called '**cash at bank**') is an **asset** and so will always be a **debit**.

  Money owed to the bank, eg a **bank loan** or an **overdraft** is a **liability** and so will always be a **credit**.

- **VAT account**   VAT account records Value Added Tax due to, or due from, HMRC (HM Customs & Revenue), ie the tax authorities.

  VAT **due to HMRC** = a **credit** balance

  VAT **due from HMRC** = a **debit** balance

some other debits and credits to remember . . .

Here are some other debit and credit account balances which you will need to remember. They all follow the basic DEAD CLIC rules for debits and credits.

Account name	Debit (£)	Credit (£)	Comment
Discounts allowed	XXXX		a decrease in sales income = an expense
Discounts received		XXXX	reduces cost of purchases = income
Purchases	XXXX		purchases = an expense
Purchases ledger control		XXXX	total of supplier accounts = a liability
Sales		XXXX	sales = an income item
Sales ledger control	XXXX		total of customer accounts = an asset (items owed to the business)

16 Memory aids

KEEPING YOUR MEMORY FIT

The human brain is an odd organ – you can remember the most useless facts, but when it comes to complex matters such as accounting procedures the mind can go completely blank. But it is possible to train your brain.

At the beginning of this Guide there are some revision tips which suggest that you can study effectively and recall information by . . .

- **Observing**, *ie remembering what information looks like on the page, using diagrams, lists, mind-maps and colour coding. Memory is very visual.*

- **Writing** *information down, using flash cards, post-it notes, notes on a phone. It is the actual process of writing which helps to fix the information in the brain.*

- **Learning** *by regularly going through your course notes and text books. Find a 'study buddy' in your class (or online) to teach and test each other as the course progresses.*

- **Chill out** *when you get tired. Give your brain a chance to recover. Get some exercise and fresh air, work out. In the ancient world there was the saying that a fit body was usually home to a fit mind.*

- **Treats** *– promise yourself rewards when you have finished studying – meet friends, eat chocolate, have a drink, listen to music.*

exam preparation

- **Practice, practice, practice** *when preparing for your assessment.*

  Practice the questions and assessments in the Osborne Books workbooks.

  Practice the free online assessments on the Osborne Books website:

  Log on to www.osbornebooks.co.uk/elearning or scan this . . .

some aids to memory

On the next few pages are blank spaces for you to set out ways of remembering debit and credit entries. Please note that if you wish to use word prompts such as 'DEAD CLIC' **make sure first** that you understand **why** each entry goes on a particular side.

1   **Double-entry** – on which side does the entry go? Make a list on the T account format below of what type of accounts are normally debits and which are normally credits, eg purchases, sales, liabilities, assets, capital, drawings etc, etc . . .

debits	credits

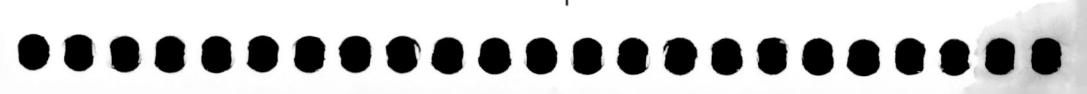

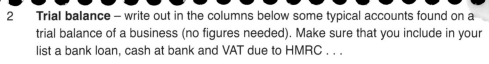

2 **Trial balance** – write out in the columns below some typical accounts found on a trial balance of a business (no figures needed). Make sure that you include in your list a bank loan, cash at bank and VAT due to HMRC . . .

debits	credits

index

notes and jottings . . .